DOLLARS AND SENSE

Developing Good Money Habits

Crabtree Publishing Company
www.crabtreebooks.com

Series Development, Writing, and Packaging:
John Burstein, Slim Goodbody Corp.

Editors:
Lynn Peppas
Valerie Weber, Wordsmith Ink.

Editorial director:
Kathy Middleton

Production coordinator:
Ken Wright

Prepress technician:
Ken Wright

Designer:
Tammy West, Westgraphix LLC.

Photos:
Chris Pinchback, Pinchback Photography

Photo credits:
© iStock Photos: pages 2, 7 (bottom), 8, 10 (bottom 14, 18 (bottom), 20, 21, 23 (middle), 24, 25
© Shutterstock: pages 4 (bottom), 26 (top)
© Slim Goodbody: pages 1, 4 (top), 6, 7 (top), 9, 10 (top), 11, 14 (middle), 17, 18 (top), 19, 22, 23 (top, bottom), 26, 27, 28 (bottom), 29

Acknowledgements:
The author would like to thank the following people for their help in this project:
Christine Burstein, Lucas Burstein, Tristan Fong, Jessie Goodale, Adriana Goodale, Colby Hill, Ginn Laurita, Louis Laurita, Renaissance Lyman, Jack Henry Grannis-Phoenix, Ariel Power, Joah Welt

Library and Archives Canada Cataloguing in Publication

Burstein, John
Dollars and sense : developing good money habits / John Burstein.

(Slim Goodbody's life skills 101)
Includes index.
Issued also in an electronic format.
ISBN 978-0-7787-4794-9 (bound).--ISBN 978-0-7787-4810-6 (pbk.)

1. Children--Finance, Personal--Juvenile literature. 2. Money--Juvenile literature. 3. Finance, Personal--Juvenile literature. I. Title. II. Title: Developing good money habits. III. Series:°Burstein, John. Slim Goodbody's life skills 101.

HG179.B883 2011 j332.0240083 C2010-902759-0

Library of Congress Cataloging-in-Publication Data

Burstein, John.
Dollars and sense : developing good money habits / John Burstein.
p. cm. -- (Slim Goodbody's life skills 101)
Includes index.
ISBN 978-0-7787-4810-6 (pbk. : alk. paper) -- ISBN 978-0-7787-4794-9 (reinforced library binding : alk. paper) -- ISBN 978-1-4271-9532-6 (electronic (pdf))
1. Children--Finance, Personal--Juvenile literature. 2. Money--Juvenile literature. 3. Finance, Personal--Juvenile literature. I. Title. II. Series.

HG179.B867 2011
332.0240083--dc22

2010016402

Crabtree Publishing Company
www.crabtreebooks.com 1-800-387-7650

Printed in China/082010/AP20100512

Published in Canada
Crabtree Publishing
616 Welland Ave.
St. Catharines, Ontario
L2M 5V6

Published in the United States
Crabtree Publishing
PMB 59051
350 Fifth Avenue, 59th Floor
New York, New York 10118

Published in the United Kingdom
Crabtree Publishing
Maritime House
Basin Road North, Hove
BN41 1WR

Published in Austra
Crabtree Publishin
386 Mt. Alexander Rd.
Ascot Vale (Melbourne
VIC 3032

CONTENTS

Words in **bold** are defined in the glossary on page 30.

MONEY TROUBLES?

Sam was thrilled when he opened the mail. His grandmother had sent him two crisp $20.00 bills for his birthday.

The first thing Sam did was to call his grandma and thank her.

"What are you going to do with the money?" Grandma asked.

"I don't know," said Sam. "There's a new hat I want to buy, and a DVD, and a cool wallet, and a video game, and..."

"Hold on, Sam," said his grandmother. "You can't afford to buy all of those things with $40.00."

"I know," replied Sam. "I guess I'll just have to think about it."

When the phone call ended, Sam went to his room to think. But the more he thought, the more confused he got.

Finally, he went to speak to his older sister Latisha about his troubles. Latisha smiled and said, "I can solve your problem."

Sam perked up. "You can? How? What should I do?"

Latisha laughed as she said, "Lend the $40.00 to me. Then you won't have to worry about what to do."

"Grrrr," growled Sam as he stormed out of his sister's room. "I almost wish I hadn't gotten the money in the first place!"

Hi. My name is Slim Goodbody.

Dealing with money can be difficult. As you get older, you will be faced with many challenging choices. You'll have to figure out how to

- **earn money**
- **spend it**
- **save it**
- **borrow it**
- **lend it**

You will be dealing with money your whole life. Money will provide you with the chance to have things and to do things. **Managing** your money is an important life skill. Good **management** will help you keep more of the money you earn and do more with the money you have.

You may not have a lot of your own money right now. Don't let that stop you from learning about handling money. It takes time to develop money-management skills. If you start now, you'll be confident about managing your money by the time you're an adult.

INCOME

Let's think about how you get money. A kid's money usually comes from several sources:

- an **allowance** given by your parents or **guardians**
- working for others
- running your own business
- gifts, such as birthday money from a relative

The money you receive is called "income." Income is simply the word for money that "comes in."

Turning Money In

From time to time, you may find money that others have lost. If you spot a coin or two lying on the sidewalk, it's OK to keep it. If you find a wallet on the sidewalk or in school, however, it does not belong to you. Bring it to your parent or teacher.

Dealing with an Allowance

Kids get most of their income from an allowance. You may wonder if most families give the same amount of money to children at different ages. For example, do most twelve-year-olds receive $5.00 per week? The answer is no. Different families deal with allowances in different ways. The best way for your family to figure out a fair allowance for you is to sit down and talk it over. Start by thinking about how much money you really need and how much you want.

"Needs" include things that are important, such as food and clothing. Your parents probably take care of most of your needs. But they might not pay for other things that you need, such as fees for class trips.

"Wants" are things that you'd like to have, but you'll still be fine if you don't get them. For example, you might want video games or a certain brand of athletic shoes.

There is nothing wrong with having wants. But when you talk about your allowance, you should ask for an amount that is fair to you and your family. You won't know what's fair if you confuse your wants with your needs.

JOBS FOR KIDS

If you want to increase your income, you can earn money by working. Of course, you will need your parents' **permission**. If they agree, here are some jobs you can look into:

1. Being a mother's helper for the younger children of friends and neighbors
2. Walking your neighbor's dog
3. Feeding your neighbors' pets while the owners are at work or on vacation
4. Doing yard work, such as raking leaves, pulling weeds, planting flowers, or shoveling snow
5. Helping in a family business by **filing** papers, mailing letters, and doing other office work
6. Opening an **organic** fruit-juice stand on a hot summer day

You can try out different jobs by agreeing to work for only short periods of time at first. Then if you don't enjoy one job, you can move on to something new.

What Should I Be Paid?

If you take a job, you need to know how much to charge. You are trading your skill and time for your **customers'** money. If you charge too little, you won't be fair to yourself. If you charge too much, you may not get hired. The solution is to determine the "going rate."

The going rate is how much other kids usually get paid for the same work. There is no one right answer because everyone's skill levels are different. For example, someone who has been babysitting for a couple of years has experience. That person can expect to be paid more than someone just starting out who has no experience.

You can figure out a fair rate by checking around your neighborhood. Talk with other kids doing similar work, and ask friends and neighbors. Look at **community** bulletin boards with ads for work to get a good idea of what jobs pay.

WHAT NOW?

Having your own money is a great thing, but it also means you have to make choices about how to use it. For example, you can

- spend it all
- save it all
- spend some
- save some
- give some away

A Word about Saving

When you're young, it's sometimes hard to think about what you'll want in the years ahead. People's goals change as they grow up. For example, when you get older, you might decide to go to college or maybe travel the world. If you begin to a save a little bit now, you'll be better able to afford to pay for those goals in the future.

Step by Step

You can take a series of steps to help you manage your money well. Take your time as you go through these steps. Make sure you understand the information given. If you have questions, speak to your parents, teacher, or other trusted adult.

Step 1: Understand Cash Flow

To make good money decisions, you need to take a close look at your "cash flow." Cash flow is a term that describes the movement of money. Sometimes money flows in. That is the income we have already talked about. Sometimes money flows out. That money is called "expenses." Your expenses are what it costs you to do the things that you want and need to do.

Together, income and expenses make up your cash flow. The best way to understand your cash flow is to keep track of all your income and all your expenses.

Keeping track of this information is not hard. Most of the facts you need are already at your fingertips. You just need to keep a carefully written record.

STEP 2: KEEP A JOURNAL

For the next month, keep track of your cash flow by creating a Cash Flow Journal in a notebook.

1. Write the month, week, and year at the top.

2. Make four columns and label each as shown.

3. Under "INCOME SOURCE," list all the ways you get money.

4. Under "INCOME AMOUNT," write down how much you get from each source in a week.

5. Add your income amounts together. Enter this sum where it says "INCOME TOTAL."

AUGUST 1-7, 2011

INCOME SOURCE	INCOME AMOUNT
Allowance	$6.00
Weekly babysitting	$9.00
Walking neighbor's dog after school	$5.00
INCOME TOTAL	$20.00

6. Under "EXPENSES," list your fixed expenses. Fixed expenses are things you have to pay for regularly. They can't be changed easily.

7. Write down the cost of each fixed expense.

8. Add your fixed expenses together and enter them next to "EXPENSES TOTAL."

9. Subtract your fixed expenses total from your income total. This total is the amount that remains for your other expenses.

EXPENSES	EXPENSES AMOUNT
School lunch	$10.00
Bus fare	$5.00
EXPENSES TOTAL	$15.00

INCOME TOTAL - EXPENSES TOTAL = $5

If you have more income than fixed expenses, you'll have some money left over. You get to decide what to do with that money.

STEP 3: MAKE A WISH LIST

Imagine that you've finished reviewing your Cash Flow Journal. You discover you have money left over! Now what will you do? To help you make the best decision, make a wish list.

1. Make two columns on a blank page in your Cash Flow notebook. Label each column as shown.

MY WISHES	MY COSTS
New bike	$150.00
Concert ticket	$20.00
iPod	$135.00
Baseball ticket	$35.00
Pizza with friends	$8.00
Brand-name athletic shoes	$120.00
Movie ticket	$10.00
Bike helmet	$40.00
TOTAL=	$518.00

2. Under "MY WISHES," write down all the things you might want to do or buy that cost money.

3. Now that you know what you want, figure out how much each item costs. Under "MY COSTS," fill in the amount next to each item. Ask an adult for help figuring out how much items cost.

4. When you know all the costs, add them up and put the number next to "TOTAL." Figure out if you have enough money to buy everything you wish for right now.

You probably won't be able to afford many things right away. Most people can't do or have everything they want.

If you don't have enough money, then you must make choices. You don't have to cross something off your list just yet. You need to get organized.

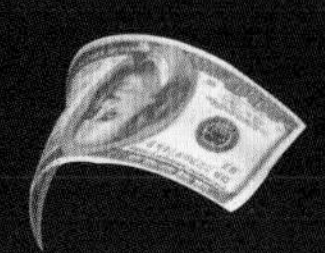

STEP 4: CHOOSE TO SPEND NOW OR LATER

Here is the best way to get organized. Think about what you want to spend your money on now and what you want to save it for later. You will need to rewrite your wish list.

1. Make one large column labeled "SHORT-TERM GOALS." These goals are things you hope to do or buy soon.

2. Make two smaller columns under "SHORT-TERM GOALS." Label them "ITEM" and "PRICE."

3. Make a second large column labeled "LONG-TERM GOALS." Long-term goals take longer because the item you want is usually expensive.

4. Under "LONG-TERM GOALS," make two smaller columns called "ITEM" and "PRICE." Divide your list of wishes between short-term and long-term goals. Put down the cost of the item too.

SHORT-TERM GOALS

ITEM	PRICE
Concert ticket	$20.00
Baseball ticket	$35.00
Pizza with friends	$ 8.00
Movie ticket	$10.00

LONG-TERM GOALS

ITEM	PRICE
New bike	$150.00
iPod	$135.00
Name-brand athletic shoes	$120.00
Bike helmet	$ 40.00

You already know you can't afford everything on the list. But don't get discouraged. We aren't finished. It's time to take the next step.

Step 5: Put Your Goals in Order

Copy the items from your wish list in the order of their **priority**. List the item you want most first, then list the item you want second, and so on.

SHORT-TERM GOALS	
ITEM	PRICE
Movie ticket	$10.00
Pizza with friends	$ 8.00
Baseball ticket	$35.00
Concert ticket	$20.00

LONG-TERM GOALS	
ITEM	PRICE
Bike helmet	$ 40.00
iPod	$135.00
New bike	$150.00
Name-brand athletic shoes	$120.00

This ordering may take some hard thinking, but you need to decide

- which one you want the most;
- what wish you are willing to give up now to get what you want later.

There is a cost to every decision. If you decide to save, be sure you think about which wishes you have to give up. Once you have decided what you want, you have to figure out how to save up the money to buy it.

STEP 6: MAKE A PLAN

Now that you know which item you want to buy first, you have a goal. It's time to plan how you will reach that goal.

1. Review your Cash Flow Journal. It shows how much you can save every week.

2. Divide the cost of the helmet by how much you can save each week.

3. Now you have your answer. It will take 8 weeks to save enough money to buy the helmet.

Let's say you want a new bike helmet that costs $40.00.

INCOME TOTAL - EXPENSES TOTAL = $5

COST OF HELMET ÷ WEEKLY SAVINGS
$40.00 ÷ $5.00 = 8

Number of weeks to save
8 weeks = $40.00

Having a plan means that you'll have the money you need to buy what you want.

Here are few suggestions for increasing your savings:

1. Start saving now. Begin with whatever money you have. No matter what the amount, it all helps.

2. Save for the future. It's important to set money aside for items you may not know about right now but may want later.

3. Make it a habit. Try to save money every single week. Think of saving as a regular expense. Tell yourself that the $20.00 you're trying to save every month is something you must do. Each time you get some money, set aside a part of it, no matter what.

4. Cut **unnecessary** expenses. For example, suppose you spend $2.00 every week on candy, soft drinks, and chips. The cost of those snacks adds up to $104.00 a year. It's probably a better idea to put that $104.00 toward something on your wish list.

5. Avoid late fees. Return things on time. You're wasting your money if you pay library fines or overdue game and video rental fees.

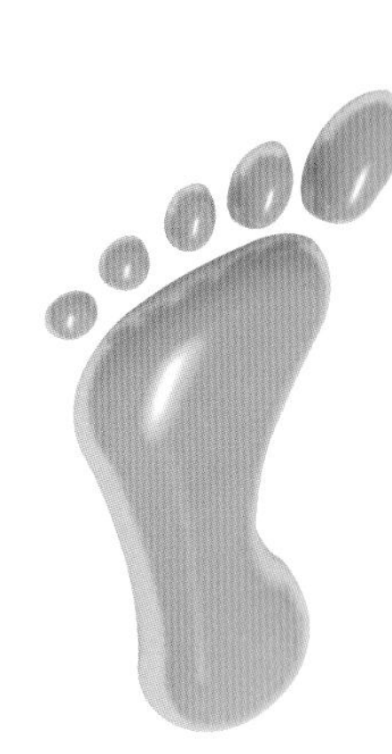

STEP 7: DECIDE WHERE TO SAVE

Once you decide how much money you're going to save, you need to decide where to keep it. You could save money

- in a piggy bank
- under your mattress
- in a safe
- in a bank

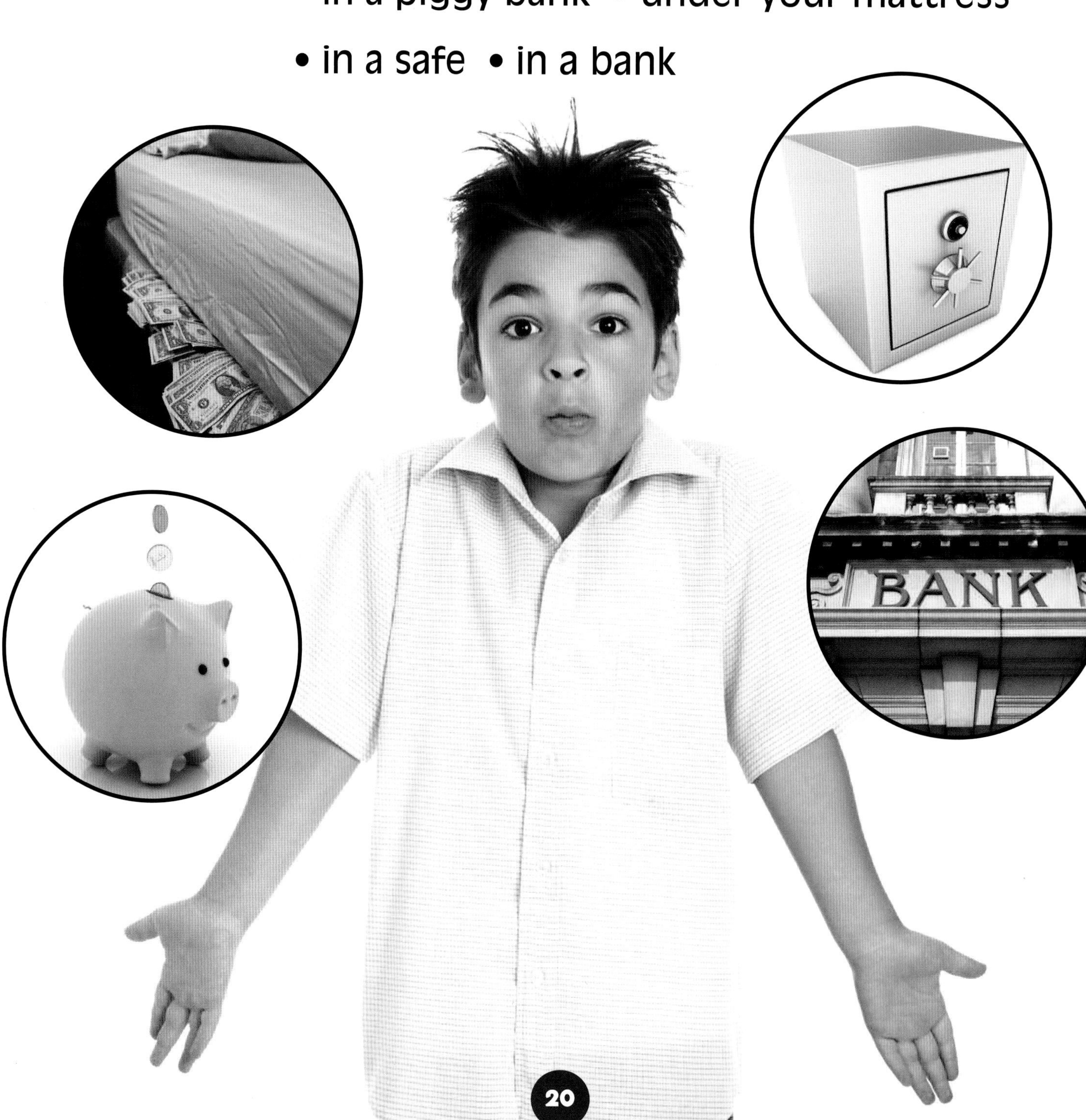

An INTERE$Ting Place To Save

You can start by putting your money in a piggy bank or some safe container at home. If you have more than a few dollars, however, a bank is the best place for that money. Here's why:

- If you keep cash at home, you're more likely to spend it. Sometimes it's hard not to buy things you want, even if they're not part of your plan. With less money at home, you'll be less likely to spend it on things you really don't need.
- The bank will pay you money for saving with them! This money is called "**interest**." Interest means that your money makes money.

You don't have to do any work at all to earn interest. If you put $100.00 in a bank one day, you will have a tiny bit more than $100.00 the next day. Day by day, the bank pays you a little more, and your money continues to grow.

You may wonder why a bank would pay you interest. The reason is this. When you save in a bank, you are really lending the bank your money. The bank can use your money to make loans to other people. The bank charges others more interest on loans than the interest they pay out to you!

STEP 8: OPEN A SAVINGS ACCOUNT

A parent or guardian will need to help you open a savings account in a bank. This account will help keep your money safe and separate from other money in the bank. When the account is opened, you fill out a "**deposit** slip." This deposit slip tells the bank how much you are putting into your savings account. The bank teller takes your money along with the deposit slip.

The teller records your deposit in a computer and gives you a slip of paper stating how much money you deposited. You also get a small book that you get to keep. This book is called a passbook. Every time you deposit money or take money out, the amount will be added to your passbook. The interest you earn will also be recorded.

ATM's

The initials ATM stand for Automatic Teller Machine. With your parents' help, you may be able to use an ATM to deposit and take out money.

Checks

Kids aren't allowed to write checks. But when you grow up, you will probably use checks. So let's learn a little bit more about how checking works.

To use a check, you must first open a special kind of bank account. It's called a checking account. Let's say you put $100.00 in the checking account. This money is not meant for saving. You are just storing it with the bank **temporarily**. The bank then gives you a checkbook that contains a certain number of checks.

When you pay for something by writing a check, the person you write the check to comes to the bank and "cashes" it. He gives the check to the bank, and the bank takes money from your checking account and gives it to him. When you write a check, it uses up money in your account. Once you've written $100.00 worth of checks, you can't write any more checks until you put more money into your checking account.

OTHER WAYS TO PAY

Online Checking

People can also pay bills online using their computers. First they log on to the company's Web site. Then they can transfer money from their checking or savings accounts at the bank directly to that company.

Debit Cards

Debit cards work a lot like checks. A debit card is a rectangular piece of plastic the bank gives you. It has your name on it along with your own private numbers. You also get a "**pin number**" that you have to remember. You need both the card and the pin number to buy something. When you use a debit card to pay for items, the money for those **purchases** is taken out of your checking account at the bank right away.

Credit Cards

A credit card looks like a debit card, but it is very different. A credit card allows you to borrow money to buy things. When you purchase something, you give the store your credit card to copy your name and private numbers. The credit card company pays the bill.

That may sound good, but at the end of the month you get a bill for all the items paid for with the credit card. If you don't pay the entire bill, the credit card company charges you a lot of interest. For example, suppose you buy something that costs $100.00. If you don't pay the amount back right away, you will be charged interest for that month. Then next month, if you still don't pay it back, not only will you be charged interest again on the $100.00, but also on last month's interest charge! On top of that, if you don't pay your bill on time, you will be charged a late fee. The money you pay back is usually much more than what you would have paid if you had used cash. With credit cards, you must be careful that you don't borrow more than you can repay right away.

STEP 9: BE A WISE BUYER

What's the key to being a smart buyer? It's really about thinking before you spend. Here are some wise spending tips:

- Before you go shopping, make a list of exactly what you want to buy. If you don't, you may forget something or buy something that isn't part of your plan.
- Do your shopping homework. A shopping list is only the starting point. Check out newspapers and flyers for sales on items on your list. Compare the **advertised** prices to see which store offers the best deal.
- Be a **bargain** hunter. If there is something you want, see if it is on sale somewhere. Look for other kinds of bargains, too. For example, if you go to a movie in the afternoon when tickets are half-price, you'll be able to go twice as often for the same cost.

- Learn about the things you are going to buy. For example, are the skates you want well-built? Are there other skates that are just as good but cost less? Are you paying more just to own a brand with a cool name?

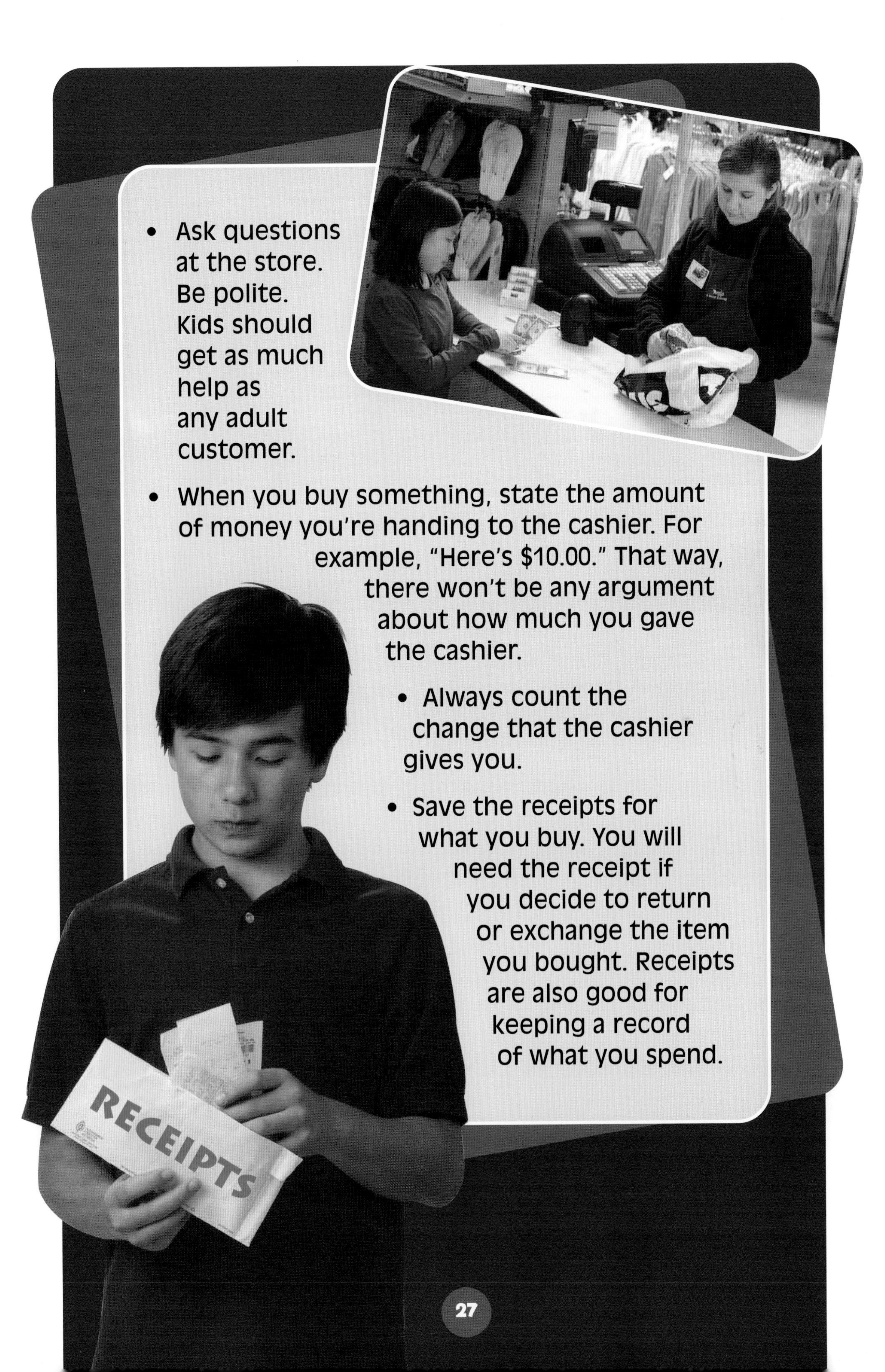

- Ask questions at the store. Be polite. Kids should get as much help as any adult customer.
- When you buy something, state the amount of money you're handing to the cashier. For example, "Here's $10.00." That way, there won't be any argument about how much you gave the cashier.
- Always count the change that the cashier gives you.
- Save the receipts for what you buy. You will need the receipt if you decide to return or exchange the item you bought. Receipts are also good for keeping a record of what you spend.

TRUE WEALTH

My whole book has been about how to manage your money. But before ending, I want to remind you that while money is useful, there are limits to what it can buy.

- Money can't buy happiness.
- Money can't buy health.
- Money can't buy love.
- Money can't buy self-respect.
- Money can't make you a better person.

Sharing Your Money: Charity

As you learn how to manage your money, please keep charity in mind. Charity means sharing with others. If you have money to spare, it is important to share a little with those less fortunate. You don't have to give a lot. Every little bit helps. Speak with your parents about charities. Charities are organizations that are specially set up to help people in need. For example, some of the charities in your community might be:

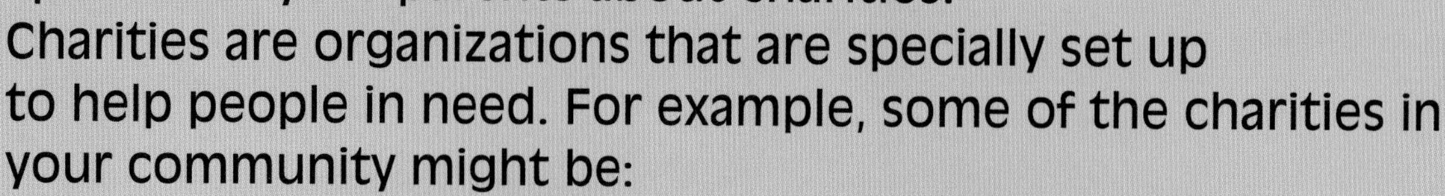

• UNICEF • soup kitchens
• food banks • the Red Cross

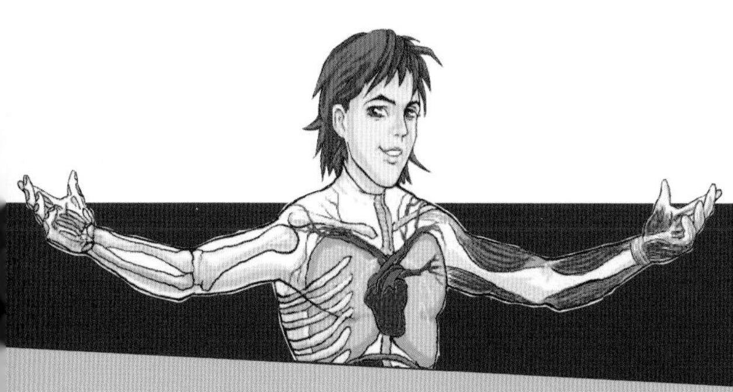

Now You Know

Practice the following steps, and you will become a better money manager:

STEP 1: UNDERSTAND CASH FLOW

STEP 2: KEEP A JOURNAL

STEP 3: MAKE A WISH LIST

STEP 4: CHOOSE TO SPEND NOW OR LATER

STEP 5: PUT YOUR GOALS IN ORDER

STEP 6: MAKE A PLAN

STEP 7: DECIDE WHERE TO SAVE

STEP 8: OPEN A SAVINGS ACCOUNT

STEP 9: BE A WISE BUYER

Learning to manage money is a skill that will help you throughout your life. Developing these good money skills makes dollars and sense.

GLOSSARY

advertised Describes products or services shown in different kinds of media, including television, radio, the Internet, magazines, and newspapers

allowance A set amount of money given at a regular time

bargain Something offered for sale or bought at a low price

community A group of people who live together in the same area

customers People who buy goods or services, such as babysitting, from someone else

deposit Describes putting money in a bank or other safe place

filing Organizing files or papers in alphabetical order

guardians People who take care of a child or someone who is not able to care for himself or herself

interest Money that is paid for the use of a larger sum of money

management The act of handling or controlling something

managing Being in charge of something

organic Describes fruits and vegetables grown without using chemicals

permission Agreement to let someone do something

pin number A short number that only the person using the debit card and his or her bank knows. A pin number allows access to a checking account.

priority Something that is more important to someone than other things

purchases Items that someone buys

temporarily Something used or lasting for only a short time

unnecessary Not needed

FOR MORE INFORMATION

BOOKS

Bair, Sheila. *Rock, Brock, and the Savings Shock.* Albert Whitman & Company

Bochner, Arthur, and Rose Bochner. *The New Totally Awesome Money Book for Kids.* Newmarket

Godfrey, Neale S. *Neale S. Godfrey's Ultimate Kids' Money Book.* Simon & Schuster Children's Publishing

Harman, Hollis Page. *Money $ense for Kids!* Barron's Educational Series

Sember, Brette McWhorter. *The Everything Kids' Money Book: Earn it, save it, and watch it grow!* Adams Media

Croke, Liam. *I'm Broke! The Money Handbook* Crabtree Publishing Company

WEB SITES

KidsBank
www.kidsbank.com
This site will help you learn how savings, interest, checking, and other banking services work.

Kids' Money for Kids
www.kidsmoney.org/kids.htm
This site offers loads of information, including a question and answer page. You can even ask questions of your own.

The Mint
www.themint.org/kids/index.html
Kids can explore earning, spending, saving, and giving money on this fun site. You can take the "Be Your Own Boss" challenge.

INDEX

About the Author
John Burstein (also known as Slim Goodbody) has been entertaining and educating children for over thirty years. His programs have been broadcast on CBS, PBS, Nickelodeon, USA, and Discovery. He has won numerous awards including the Parent's Choice Award and the President's Council's Fitness Leader Award. Currently, Mr. Burstein tours the country with his multimedia live show "Bodyology." For more information, please visit **slimgoodbody.com**.